P9-DBT-470

Juan Ponce de León

and the Search for the Fountain of Youth

Explorers of New Worlds

Daniel Boone and the Exploration of the Frontier
Christopher Columbus and the Discovery of the New World
Francisco Coronado and the Exploration of the American Southwest
Hernando Cortés and the Conquest of Mexico
Lewis and Clark: Explorers of the Louisiana Purchase
Vasco da Gama and the Portuguese Explorers
Ferdinand Magellan and the First Voyage Around the World
Marco Polo and the Wonders of the East
Juan Ponce de León and the Search for the Fountain of Youth
Hernando de Soto and the Exploration of Florida

Juan Ponce de León

and the Search for the Fountain of Youth

Dan Harmon

Chelsea House Publishers
Philadelphia

Prepared for Chelsea House Publishers by:
OTTN Publishing, Warminster PA

CHELSEA HOUSE PUBLISHERS
Editor in Chief: Stephen Reginald
Managing Editor: James D. Gallagher
Production Manager: Pamela Loos
Art Director: Sara Davis
Director of Photography: Judy L. Hasday
Senior Production Editor: LeeAnne Gelletly
Series Designer: Keith Trego

First Printing
1 3 5 7 9 8 6 4 2

Library of Congress Cataloging-in-Publication Data

Harmon, Dan.
   Juan Ponce de León and the search for the Fountain of
   Youth / by Dan Harmon.
p.   cm. – (Explorers of new worlds)
Includes bibliographical references and index.
Summary: A biography of the Spanish explorer and gov-
ernor of Cuba, who attempted to find the Fountain of
Youth in the New World.
ISBN 0-7910-5517-5 (hc)
1. Ponce de León, Juan, 1460?–1521 Juvenile literature.
2. Explorers–America Biography Juvenile literature. 3.
Explorers–Spain–Biography Juvenile literature.   4.
America–Discovery and exploration–Spanish Juvenile
literature. [1. Ponce de León, Juan, 1460?–1521. 2.
Explorers.   3. America–Discovery and exploration–
Spanish.] I. Title. II. Series.
E125.P7H37   1999
972.9'02'092–dc21   99-22260
[B]   CIP

Contents

1 The Dying Conquistador 7

2 A Humble Lad
Becomes a Soldier 11

3 To the New World
with Columbus 21

4 The Soldier
Becomes a Planter 29

5 An Island of
Endless Youth? 41

6 The Last Expedition 51

Chronology 59

Glossary 60

Further Reading 62

Index 63

The Dying
Conquistador

Juan Ponce de León's men test the water in Florida to see if they have found the mythical Fountain of Youth. Ponce's search for the legendary fountain failed, as did his attempt to develop a Spanish colony in Florida in the early 16th century.

I

he burning! Such agony! Can no one stop the burning?
In the cabin of a small ship, one of the most famous Spanish explorers lay mortally wounded. His thigh, pierced by an Indian's arrow, was painfully inflamed and infected. Poison already had spread through his bloodstream.

The victim was being transported from the coast of Florida, where his landing party had been attacked, to

Havana, a new Spanish settlement in Cuba. There, his men hoped, he could be treated successfully. But even if they reached shore in time, there was little doctors in the year 1521 could do. The groaning man undoubtedly knew he soon would die.

But how could this be? Juan Ponce de León had discovered the Florida coast eight years before, in 1513. Spain's King Ferdinand himself had appointed Ponce governor of the new land. How could a territorial governor be dying from the wound of a primitive weapon?

Ponce de León was no ordinary governor. He was first and foremost a soldier and explorer. Even though he had accumulated enough wealth to live very comfortably, Ponce was determined to find, settle and explore new islands. The life of a **conquistador** had always been dangerous. He was used to danger.

Until now, however, Ponce always had been the victor. He had fought Taino and Carib tribes on the islands of Hispaniola and Borinquen (Puerto Rico) for many years. He was one of Spain's best military leaders in the New World. In fact, it was his military **prowess** that had earned him positions of leadership on these islands.

Florida was different—much different. The natives there had heard about the men who came in sailing ships with shining armor and strange, powerful weapons. They apparently knew how native tribes on the islands to the southeast had been beaten, raped, forced to work, sent off in chains across the ocean, and brutally slaughtered.

From the day Ponce de León first landed in Florida, he had found the Indians there determined to resist. They refused to make friends with the Spaniards. They tried to lure the invaders into ambushes. Finally, the Floridians had succeeded in bringing down the leader of these unwanted visitors.

Thoughts about his family, memories of past glory, sorrow over grand plans he never would see carried out—all of these must have passed through Ponce's mind as the ship approached Havana. But above all was the terrible pain and fever. . . .

Howe a man schall be armyd at his ese
when he schal fighte on foote

He schal haue noo schurte vp on him but a
dowbelet of ffustean lynyd wyth satene cutte
full of hoolis. the dowbelet muste be strongeli boūdē
there the poyntis muste be sette aboute the greet of the
arme. and the b ste before and behynde and the gussetis
tis of mayle muste be sowid vn to the dowbelet in
the bought of the arme. and vndir the arme the ar
mynge poyntis muste be made of fyne twyne suche
as men make stryngis for crossebowes and they

A Humble Lad Becomes a Soldier

2

No one can be certain when or where Juan Ponce de León was born. His birth probably occurred between 1460 and 1474. This would have been 20 or 30 years before Columbus's first voyage across the sea to what would become known as the New World.

Some historians believe Ponce's hometown was San Servos in the Spanish *province* of León. (A province is a geographical area, similar to a U.S. state.) One of his ancestors may have married an important person from this province in northwestern Spain. Thus "de León" was added to the family name. (In Spanish, "de León" means "of León." If your name is John Alexis and you come from León, you might be called John Alexis de León.)

Spain at this time in history was a country of warring nobles fighting each other for power and honor. Catholicism was the only religion that was allowed. In 1478, Pope Sixtus, the leader of the Catholic church, established what became known as the **Spanish Inquisition**. It was a movement to purge the country of **infidels**, people who were not sincere in their Catholic beliefs. Over the next 300 years, thousands of Jews, Muslims, and Protestants were executed by the Spanish Inquisition. Attacks on non-Christians were common in other European countries, too. But in Spain the Inquisition was extremely well organized and aggressively enforced by the Spanish rulers. Its abuses were terrible.

Ponce came from a long line of Spanish nobility, but his family had fallen on hard times. Both of his parents died young. Some biographers think Ponce de León may have been raised by a great-aunt.

He seemed to be facing a bleak, hard life. But fortunately, as a teenager he was able to join the service of a Spanish knight, Don Pedro Núñez de Guzmán. Don Pedro was a friend of the Spanish

A court of priests and religious leaders discusses the fate of men accused by the Spanish Inquisition. During this period, people who did not conform to Christian religious beliefs were often tortured or killed.

royal family. Over the years, Don Pedro would become like a father to young Ponce, and his royal connection would prove very valuable.

Ponce began service in Don Pedro's household as a lowly ***page***. He was expected to perform many daily chores: gathering up the dirty clothes, setting the table for meals, making sure the home was always clean and everything was in its proper place, tending the candles, and bringing wood for the hearths. In return for his work, Ponce was given a home and an education. In 15th-century Spain, this included learning how to become a soldier.

Every page understandably wanted to advance to a more important role in life. Each dreamed of becoming a **squire**. It was as a squire that he would begin to learn the art of combat. Squires went to the battlefields as shield and armor bearers for the knights they served. Meanwhile, they themselves were learning to use swords and lances. They were learning to fight on horseback.

Don Pedro watched Ponce very quickly outgrow his duties as a page. Ponce clearly was a fast learner and was willing to obey orders instantly. Don Pedro was so impressed that he made Ponce his personal squire, and ordered that he begin training to fight.

Thus Juan Ponce de León became a soldier. Some young men of noble backgrounds would have scoffed at the idea of becoming an ordinary soldier. But Ponce was pleased. His life and fame would be based on his ability as a fighting man.

Don Pedro, Ponce's kind benefactor, had more respect for Ponce than for the other soldiers in his

This picture, taken from a painting in a Spanish castle, shows knights training in a tournament. It was at competitions such as this that young Spanish squires practiced their fighting skills.

army. His admiration soon proved well placed. When Spain went to war with neighboring Portugal, Ponce had his first real chance to demonstrate his fighting knowledge and his leadership ability. At the Battle of Toro, Ponce fought so well that King Ferdinand knighted him. He became a captain under Don Pedro's command.

The common soldiers considered Ponce de León a good captain. Ponce had been a regular soldier himself, so he understood the men who served under him: how they thought, how they should be treated. In return, he was among the most-respected officers in the army.

Soon after Spain defeated Portugal, Ponce found himself at war again. King Ferdinand and Queen Isabella began a long campaign to drive the **Moors** from Granada, a province in southern Spain that borders the Mediterranean Sea. In that province, a southern city that was also called Granada was the Moors' last great stronghold in Spain.

The Moors were Arabs from northern Africa. In 711 A.D., they had invaded and overrun southern Spain. To drive the Moors out, Ferdinand and Isabella united the Spanish lords, who had been fighting each other. All the noblemen's armies now joined to oppose one common enemy.

Don Pedro, of course, would have been in the thick of the campaign–along with his trusted captain, Juan Ponce de León. For 10 years, the Spaniards very slowly, castle by castle, took back the lands from the Moors. The last of the Moors in Spain surrendered in 1492. In that same year, an

Italian navigator and dreamer named Christopher Columbus discovered tropical islands far, far away to the west.

The king rewarded the aging Don Pedro for his faithful service against the Moors. He appointed him to teach his son, Prince Charles, at the royal palace. Ponce stayed in Granada with the Spanish army.

Columbus, meanwhile, had created much excitement when he returned from the islands he called the "Indies" in 1493. He had made the voyage for Spain hoping to find a westward ocean passage to China, Japan, and other lands of Asia that were called the East Indies. It was not until a few years later that people realized that Columbus had, in fact, found new lands. The islands he discovered eventually became known as the West Indies.

On his return, however, Columbus astounded the Spanish royal court with products from the islands and with fascinating, colorfully costumed natives who came back with him. He presented exotic birds to the king and queen. He also displayed a small quantity of gold.

The quest for gold, *spices*, and other riches was the main reason most Spaniards were interested in exploration. (Queen Isabella also wanted to convert foreign cultures to Christianity.) Columbus and his men had found very little gold—just jewelry the Indians wore for ornamentation and a few nuggets found in the island creeks and rivers. Columbus wanted to return to the islands for further exploration, however. So he convinced the king that much gold yet might be found on the large island that he had named *La Isla Española* ("the Spanish Isle"). On this island, which eventually became known as Hispaniola, Columbus had left a small settlement: a crude fort occupied by about 40 men.

The excited Spanish court approved his plans for a second expedition. This one would be protected by a small army as it attempted to establish a colony in the New World.

How Ponce came to join the great expedition is not recorded. But it seems safe to speculate that his old mentor Don Pedro had much to do with it. Don Pedro would have known the young fighter was unhappy and bored serving in Granada, where the fighting was over. He probably decided to do Ponce a great favor.

Spain at this time was filled with professional soldiers who had little to do, for the country was at peace after the Moors were defeated. Thousands of fighting men clamored for a chance to search for gold and adventure in the New World. As Columbus prepared for his next expedition, his biggest problem was not a shortage of willing volunteers, but too many of them!

It was in this situation that Don Pedro probably used his special influence at court on Ponce's behalf. He persuaded the expedition's organizers to include Ponce as one of the soldiers on Columbus' second voyage to the New World.

Ponce, of course, was eager to go. Most of the people who were going to the New World dreamed of fabulous riches. But Ponce may have been more excited by the chance to go exploring.

His life was about to change dramatically. He had expected to spend his life as a professional soldier in Spain, waiting for the next battle. Now he was to become a seafarer, too. He would make his name as an explorer and conqueror of strange, distant lands—a conquistador.

To the New World with Columbus 3

On his first voyage, Columbus had been able to take only three small ships: the *Niña*, *Pinta*, and *Santa Maria*. This time he commanded a fleet of 17 vessels and more than a thousand men.

The second Columbus expedition sailed from the Spanish port of Cadiz on September 25, 1493. It was a grand occasion. Many citizens gathered to see the ships depart. Musicians performed aboard boats in the harbor. Cannons were fired from shore to salute the adventurers. Flags flew gaily in the salt breeze.

The Spanish soldiers, so valiant in land battles, now

had to confront a subtle new enemy: seasickness! Ponce set about getting his "sea legs." He had plenty of time to get used to the endless rolling and rocking of the little ship on the great ocean swells. It took several weeks to make the Atlantic crossing.

In part, they were weeks of misery. The voyagers this trip were favored with fair weather, but the time passed slowly. Food aboard old sailing ships was never very tasty, and it grew increasingly bad on long voyages. And even though Columbus had proved there was land ahead of them, there was still uncertainty. In that period, even short ocean voyages along the coasts of Europe and Africa were filled with dangers. Sailing all the way across the Atlantic was much riskier.

In the early morning of November 3, 1493, Ponce heard voices shouting, "Tierra! Tierra!"— Spanish for "Land! Land!" The lookouts had seen an island in the faint light of dawn. Ponce was about to get his first glimpse of the New World! Still in his sleeping clothes, he ran up to the ship's main deck.

In the distance, Ponce could see a low mountain rising from the water. The leaders soon realized this was not Hispaniola, where Columbus had left his settlement on his first voyage. This was part of an island chain to the southeast—islands never before seen by Europeans. Columbus claimed them for the Spainish king and queen.

The fleet sailed on to Hispaniola. When they reached Navidad, the little outpost Columbus had established the year before, they didn't find the prospering town they had expected. No cannons from shore answered their greeting signals as they approached. There was only a deserted, badly damaged fort. The remains of dead Spaniards were in the bushes nearby.

Using sign language and fragments of Spanish language, natives explained what had happened. The settlers had not established farms, as Columbus had wanted. Instead, they had spent most of their time looking for gold. They had forced the Indians to pan for it in the island streams. They had stolen the gold necklaces the Indians wore. Some of those items had been family *heirlooms*, passed down from one generation to another.

To the Indians, gold had no special value, except as shiny ornaments and family relics. Pretty seashells meant just as much to them as gold. They didn't understand why the Spaniards were so frantic to obtain it.

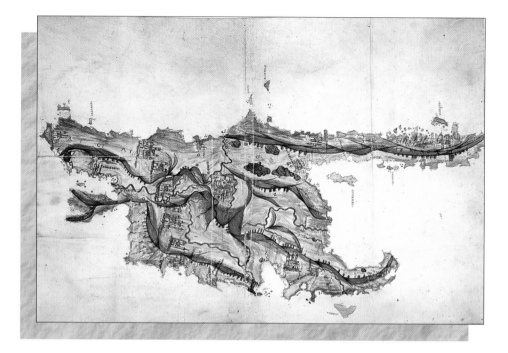

This 16th-century Spanish map shows settlements on the island of Hispaniola. Today, this island is shared by Haiti and the Dominican Republic.

In their greed, the settlers had taken every bit of gold they could get their hands on. Meanwhile, they had made the Indians tend their crops and provide them with food. In drunken fits, the Spaniards had treated the Indians with unbelievable brutality.

A few months after Columbus had returned to Spain, the situation at Navidad had become unbearable for the Indians. They had banded together under a chief named Caonabo and attacked the settlement. All of the Spaniards had been killed.

Amazingly, the Indians were still friendly to Columbus and his new expedition. Juan Ponce de León apparently respected the natives, and learned to speak their language.

But for the most part, the Spaniards were anything but friendly toward the Indians. They were forced to work in the fields and to help look for gold. It was much the same this time as the year before. When gold could not be found, some of the angry Spaniards beat the Indians and cut off their ears! Naturally, the Indians began to resist. Some of the Indian warriors were caught and hanged or burned to death.

As a Spanish soldier, Juan Ponce de León did his share of Indian fighting. This may not have been how he wanted to spend his time in the New World, but he had little choice. He probably would rather have been exploring and planting crops.

Ponce was beginning to understand that the real promise of this new territory was not in its gold, but in its fertile soil. He could envision harvesting large fields of products that could not be grown in Spain, and shipping them home for handsome profits. Columbus was building a new city, Isabela, about 75 miles from the failed settlement at Navidad. This

*W*hy did European explorers and settlers treat the natives so terribly? The Indians of the New World were friendly, at first. To the natives, these armor-clad conquistadors were like gods, to be feared and obeyed. The islanders did not want to fight them.

However, the Spaniards considered Indians to be savages, equal only to animals. The conquistadors did not understand the Indians' religious beliefs or way of living. This was the time of the Spanish Inquisition. Spaniards were executing their own citizens because of different religious beliefs. The explorers therefore had little respect for native customs.

Also, if the conquistadors converted the natives to Christianity, as the queen wanted, they would have to treat them with respect. The Spaniards decided it was better to leave the natives "wild" so that they could justify using them as slaves. The Catholic priests who came to the islands as missionaries protested this violent behavior, but they could do little to prevent it.

New World might turn out to be the best place for Ponce to spend the rest of his life.

Life here was not without hardships, though. The settlers—including Columbus—came down with strange diseases. Some of them died. (At the same time, the Spaniards were giving the Indians European diseases that could not be treated.) Progress at farming was slow. The abused natives grew increasingly unfriendly. There were problems in the colony as well. Columbus was unable to control his soldiers well. Many of the men resented Columbus because he was an Italian by birth, not a Spaniard like them.

Ponce was proving himself to be a very good soldier. He was such a good military leader that he eventually was made commander of the garrison at Santo Domingo.

He was becoming a citizen of the New World.

Explorers of New Worlds

The Soldier
Becomes
a Planter

Fields of sugarcane like this one made Juan Ponce de León a wealthy man in the New World.

4

istory has recorded almost nothing of Juan Ponce de León's activities between 1493 and 1502. His military record undoubtedly was excellent. Still, as an ordinary Spanish soldier, there was little about him to attract the notice of men writing about the New World.

In the spring of 1496, Columbus sailed back to Spain. He left most of his men behind to build a permanent colony on Hispaniola. Some historians believe Ponce returned to Spain with him and remained there for several years. Others believe he may have remained at the Hispaniola colony.

We do know that by 1502, he was married and had a family. And in that year, Don Nicolás de Ovando was appointed *viceroy*, or governor, of the settlement at Hispaniola. He arrived with 2,500 settlers aboard 30 ships.

The Spanish who were coming to the New World marveled at the exotic birds, strange animals, and unknown plant life. The native Taino people were just as fascinating. They were gentle people who lived in small villages all over the island.

Few of these Spanish newcomers realized they would have to learn a very different way of life. They had to get used to living in grass huts, sleeping in *hammocks*, and eating off palm leaves. The food here, and the way it was prepared, was unlike what they had enjoyed at home. To nobles and their servants and soldiers, who were used to the stone castles, fine clothing, and elegant traditions of Spain, it was a shock.

The Spaniards certainly were not prepared to work for a living—at least not while there were native "savages" who could be enslaved to do their work for them. Some of the Indians on the island literally were worked to death.

Most of the Spaniards had come to the Indies for only one reason: to get rich. If they failed to find gold, the Spaniards knew they could obtain money by capturing Indians and selling them as slaves back home. During the first few years of Spanish settlement, hundreds of natives were enslaved and shipped to Europe.

Ferdinand and Isabella soon forbade this practice and instituted a peculiar system called ***encomienda***. It meant the Spanish settlers could have natives as servants, but they must take care of them and teach them about Christianity. In practice, this system was very similar to outright slavery.

As for Ponce de León, he was part of the new Spanish establishment with its unfair practices. He went with raiding parties on their slave-finding raids. But he also seemed willing to work. By the time Ovando arrived, Ponce had decided to make his life in the New World. He wanted to establish a ***plantation*** and farm the rich tropical soil. He would make his fortune off the land, not by searching for gold. The native Taino were excellent farmers, and Ponce knew he could learn a lot from them.

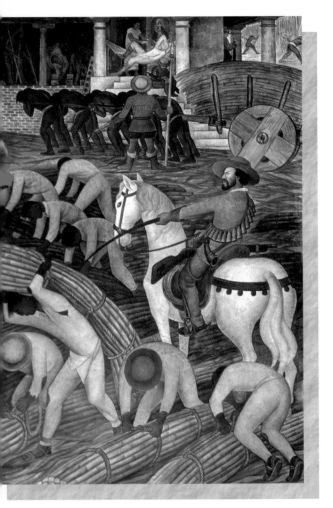

This Mexican mural shows how the Spanish mistreated the natives whom they enslaved to work the sugar plantations.

Things did not go as Ponce envisioned, however. Ovando refused to release him from the army so that he could become a farmer. The new viceroy needed experienced soldiers and officers to keep the natives under control. Although the Taino were peaceful by nature, the invaders from across the sea were bringing out the worst in them.

There were an estimated 3 million Taino on Hispaniola, compared to only a few thousand Spaniards. But the Indians couldn't wipe out these harsh, lazy Europeans because the Spaniards were much better armed. They had swords, crossbows, cannons, and crude firearms. The invaders were protected by metal armor. And the Spaniards had come prepared to fight and conquer. The Taino were armed only with spears and arrows, and they lived in tribes that did not always get along well with one another. They were not organized to attack, or even to defend themselves. They were intimidated by the Spaniards' horses—monstrous animals they never had seen before. When Indian slaves fled into the swamps, they were chased down by the Spaniards' huge, fierce dogs.

Within about 50 years, the Taino vanished completely from the island. Many were killed by the Spaniards or carried away as slaves. Thousands died of diseases brought from Europe—illnesses to which their bodies were not *immune*. Some were in such despair from the Spanish invasion that they poisoned themselves rather than become slaves.

When the natives' resistance was broken, Ponce finally was granted a plantation of his own. Ponce had earned Ovando's deep respect by helping defeat the Taino. The viceroy even made Ponce a governor, or *adelantado*, of the province of Higuey on Hispaniola. Ponce now could begin his career as a planter, and start to earn his fortune.

Although he had fought against them, Ponce apparently valued the Indians for their wisdom. He wanted to use the Indians not just for their labor, but for their advice. They knew the tropical climate and the island's soil qualities far better than any European settler.

With the Indians' help, Ponce became a successful farmer. His main crops were sugarcane and native corn, called **maize**. The Spaniards used the sugarcane to make rum, a popular form of liquor.

Ponce's lands produced many valuable food products. His workers shipped meat from his livestock herds and harvests from his fields back to Spain, where they brought good prices at market.

Thus, while other Spaniards in the New World were frustrated because they could find little gold, Ponce became wealthy. He recognized the real "gold" when he saw it: the fertile land.

But Ponce had an adventurer's heart. He still wanted to find gold for Spain in the New World, and thought it might be located on the island called Borinquen. Today, this is the island we call Puerto Rico. Although its distance from the coast of Hispaniola is about 80 miles, the natives of the two islands frequently traded with each other. It was about one day's boat journey away.

Ponce's interest in Borinquen is believed to have

Ponce de León studied the methods of the native farmers to become a successful plantation owner himself.

heightened one day when a native of the island asked to trade some yellow pebbles he had brought for a string of the Spaniards' "musical bells." The musical necklaces were merely trinkets that the Europeans had brought to the Indies for trading purposes—but to the Indians, they were prizes. On the other hand, the natives considered the island pebbles—gold!—to be just bright stones. This Indian from Borinquen had heard that the Spaniards valued the stones for some crazy reason. He was eager to make a deal.

Perhaps, thought Ponce and Ovando, the elusive gold of the New World was on Borinquen, not Hispaniola. Ovando sent Ponce across the strait on a mission with a small exploratory party to see what he could find. The trip was kept secret. If there was gold to be found on the smaller neighboring island, Ovando did not want it to become known.

Ponce and his expedition arrived at Borinquen and soon befriended a chief named Guaybana. The Spaniards indeed found gold, though not in great amounts. But it was enough to persuade King Ferdinand to let Ponce establish mines on the island—and to make him governor of Borinquen. As in Higuey, Ponce established a plantation on Borinquen and began farming, using Indian labor.

Between his plantations in Higuey and Borinquen and his share of the island's mining operation, Ponce was becoming a very rich man. He and his family lived in luxury. They had fine fabrics and tapestries brought over from Spain. Much of their furniture was hand-carved from rare wood by island natives. They rode in a grand carriage.

Ponce also seems to have been an effective, though arguably cruel, governor. Under his leader-

Ponce de León established Borinquen as an important Spanish outpost in the New World. The capital, San Juan, is protected by walls like many cities in Spain.

ship, other sugar cane plantations were established on Borinquen. Several cities were built, including the capital, San Juan.

Ponce's mark remains on Puerto Rico's history to this day. Sugarcane is still an important crop, and San Juan, a city he established, is still the island's capital. But success did not come without a price. Under the Spanish oppression, the native Taino

What was Juan Ponce de León the conquistador like? There is no question he was a bold soldier. Beyond that, we only can guess—and the theories about Ponce differ wildly.

For example, some of his biographers have pictured him as a man with a warm heart. This would have made him very different from many of the cruel, greedy Spanish explorers the Indians came to hate. These writers see Ponce as a man who respected the natives and, although he became their master, took good care of them.

Others doubt he was very different from other European invaders, who brutally beat, enslaved, and killed the natives. One historian claims that Ponce was "spoiled by ambition and envy. He governed Puerto Rico so savagely that the Indians revolted and the King recalled him."

It is difficult to know what was in the hearts of Ponce de León and other explorers from this time. Certainly, brutality was common while they were in power. Perhaps the real character of Ponce de León was somewhere between these extremes.

people of Borinquen rebelled. As on Hispaniola, the Spaniards crushed their resistance. But many men on both sides were killed. And while all this was happening, Spanish politics shook up the leadership of both islands.

In the year 1511, Ponce had been governor of Borinquen for two years. King Ferdinand replaced Viceroy Ovando at Hispaniola with Don Diego Columbus, the son of Christopher Columbus. Don Diego had inherited the royal title of governor from his father, who had died in 1506. And Don Diego now considered Ponce his political enemy, because Ponce was an friend of Ovando. So Ponce was removed as governor of Borinquen and replaced by two of Don Diego's supporters.

Fortunately for Ponce, he had a very important friend back in Spain: King Ferdinand himself. The king ordered Don Diego Columbus to let Ponce keep his plantations. Ponce also remained the military leader on Borinquen.

This relationship between Ponce and the new viceroy was an uneasy one. Although he was wealthy and respected, Ponce was restless. Why not find new islands to explore?

Juan Ponce de León probably didn't believe in the legend of the Fountain of Youth, but he never wanted to pass up an adventure, or an opportunity to find wealth in the New World.

An Island of Endless Youth?

5

*B*imini.

Juan Ponce de León let the word tumble gently through his dreams. It was mysterious . . . and exciting!

The Indians of the New World talked often about an island named Bimini. No one seemed to know its location, though. Apparently, it was one of the hundreds of islands to the northwest that the Spanish had not yet explored.

According to the Indians, the island of Bimini had a large spring coming up from the ground. If a person drank from it or swam in it, they said, the magical waters would make the person young again.

Proof was hard to find. Ponce could find no native who claimed to have been to Bimini and drunk from this "fountain of youth." He knew of no centuries-old Indians with youthful skin and perfect health. Everyone who told stories of Bimini and its mystical fountain merely talked about people they had heard about who had become young again.

Did a practical, wise old soldier like Ponce himself believe the legend? Probably not. If the story was true, why weren't the islands filled with people who appeared to be young but were actually hundreds of years old? Why could he not find a single native who would make such a claim?

Still, Ponce was curious. Historical legends about a fountain of youth went back almost 2,000 years to the time of Alexander the Great—and perhaps further. Also, he knew the Indians used herbs and other roots to treat diseases and wounds in ways the Spaniards did not understand. Could these strange islands also offer a healing stream of water?

> It is possible that the Indians got the idea of a fountain of youth from the Spaniards themselves. Maybe the Indians wanted to send the invaders in search of an island that didn't exist.

No one knows for sure what Ponce believed about this fountain of youth. Almost certainly, at any rate, he had other reasons for wanting to look for the fabled island of Bimini.

It must have occurred to Ponce and other Spaniards that if this wild legend was true, or even partly true, there was much money to be made. European aristocrats would pay fortunes for a flask of this water to be shipped back to the Old World. They would give all the gold they owned for a sip of renewed youth, would they not? The finders of the fountain could name their price!

Some historians suspect King Ferdinand was keenly interested in this fountain of youth. He was growing old; Queen Isabella had already died. If there was a way to restore youth in the New World, the king certainly would want to know about it.

To Juan Ponce de León, the idea of a search for the fountain of youth was very appealing. Ponce himself was entering middle age. But even if no such water was found, there would be new islands to conquer. Perhaps he would be named adelantado of Bimini, and there would find the gold and other riches that so far had eluded the Spanish explorers.

The year was 1513. This was the same year

another Spaniard, Vasco Núñez de Balboa, crossed the Isthmus of Panama in what is now Central America and became the first European to see the Pacific Ocean. New lands were being found and fellow countrymen winning glory while Ponce was growing older and discontented on Borinquen. He did not like serving under Don Diego Columbus.

If the fountain existed, why not find it? Even if the stories were false, they were still an excuse to go exploring one more time before he was too old.

Ponce obtained the king's blessing to make a voyage in search of Bimini. He agreed to pay all the expenses. Ponce hired an experienced navigator, Anton de Alaminos, to guide him on his journey to the unknown northwest.

His little expedition of three ships–the *Santa Maria de Consolación,* the *San Cristoval,* and the *Santiago*–sailed from Borinquen on March 3, 1513. With Ponce were young Spanish soldiers who hoped to claim new plantation grants of their own in Bimini. If necessary, they intended to take the island from its natives by force.

Ponce de León's convoy sailed northwest. In a few days, the ships reached San Salvador, the island where Columbus had first landed 21 years earlier.

hat were the ships that transported Ponce de León and his men to Florida like? Typical Spanish ocean vessels of the period were very small, by today's standards. Columbus's ship, the *Niña*, was about 70 feet long and 20 feet wide. This is shorter than a basketball court, and only about half as wide!

The *Niña* was a common type of sailing ship, called a caravel. Caravels were noted for their high, rounded bows and high, squared sterns. They looked funny and rocked uncomfortably on the ocean swells. Some had square sails, and others had lateen, or triangular, sails.

Later in the 16th century, the larger galleon became famous as the Spaniards' standard ship type for fighting and for transporting gold and other riches from the New World to Spain.

F. Delfinum

When Ponce de León and his men arrived in Florida,
he found the natives were unfriendly and ready to fight
the invaders.

There they took aboard water and supplies and repaired a leaking hull. Then they continued northwestward into unknown waters. They did not realize they were heading not for an island, but for a continent—what is today known as North America.

In late March, about three weeks after departing Borinquen, they sighted a long, low coastline. But a storm came up and blew them out into the Atlantic Ocean. It was several days before they saw land again to the west. On April 2, 1513, the lookouts sighted a coastline.

The explorers landed on a beautiful beach that was covered with shells. Inland, the lush greenery was thickened with spring flowers. The coast teemed with birds and butterflies. Today, some researchers believe the Spaniards were near the site of what would become St. Augustine–the oldest city in America today. Others suspect this landing place was several miles to the south.

Ponce and his men planted a flag on the beach and solemnly claimed the land for Spain. It was the Easter season, so Ponce called the land *Pascua Florida* (Spanish for "Easter of flowers").

There is disagreement among historians over whether this was the first time Europeans had set foot on the North American mainland. Many scholars believe the Vikings from northern Europe crossed the Atlantic centuries earlier. Certainly Ponce was the first Spaniard to do so.

Despite its beauty, Florida was far from friendly. The Spanish left their first landing site and sailed along the coast. On several occasions, Ponce tried to land and meet the Indians. The natives responded with darts and arrows! They wanted nothing to do with these Europeans. The Indians of Florida may have been warned by other natives to avoid the brutal, bearded visitors wearing glittering armor who arrived in large ships.

Ponce sailed further up the coast, then down. He was trying to get an idea of the size of this new "island." While doing so, his ships encountered the powerful Gulf Stream that flows from the Gulf of Mexico around the Florida Keys and northward into the Atlantic Ocean. The Spaniards never had experienced a powerful ocean current like this one. It could drive a vessel northward even when the wind was blowing southward!

The Spaniards sailed down the coastline all the way to where it trended westward. This was the wilderness site of what is today the sprawling area of Miami, Florida. Rounding the tip of the Florida peninsula, the explorers continued up the west coast in what is called today the Gulf of Mexico. Drawing near the shore at one point, they were attacked by a fleet of about 80 native war canoes. Cannon fire from the Spanish ships frightened away the warriors.

Just how far they sailed up the western coast of

Florida is not known. But Ponce had seen enough to convince him this was a very large island. Perhaps it was a continent!

The Spaniards had not been able to explore very far inland because of the hostile Indians. Was there gold to be found? Rich soil for plantations? Ponce would have to wait for another trip to answer these and other questions about Florida.

But one thing the Spaniards had learned about Pascua Florida: Its waters did nothing to make anyone look or feel younger.

Ponce de León and his men struggle through the forests of Florida, searching for the Fountain of Youth.

The Last Expedition 6

By the terms of his contract with King Ferdinand, Ponce was now the adelantado of Florida—which Ponce still thought to be a large island. But he had to find a way to colonize the beautiful new territory.

Ponce's men wanted to return to Borinquen, and Ponce agreed. They were having problems with the ships. There was no way the vessels could be beached and repaired properly with hostile natives likely to attack at any time. Also, by this time it was mid-June, and the mariners knew hurricanes soon would become a threat.

The ships returned to Borinquen by different routes.

One of them apparently did find the small island the Indians called Bimini in what is now the Straits of Florida. Its fresh water, unfortunately, seemed no more magical than the water on other islands.

Ponce's expedition arrived back in Borinquen in October 1513. Soon, Ponce was on his way to Spain to report his findings directly to the king. He hoped to obtain from Ferdinand a detailed contract that would give Ponce firm authority over this beautiful, gigantic new domain.

Was King Ferdinand disappointed that Ponce did not bring him magical water from the fabled fountain of youth? History does not record his reaction. The king undoubtedly was delighted by the description of lovely Florida—and by Ponce's de León 's gift of gold, which the explorer had taken from his personal treasury.

The king gave Ponce what he wanted. He agreed that Ponce would have control over the colonization of Florida, as well as over the money that would be produced from trade there. Ponce could grant trade agreements and plantations to whomever he wished. The king, of course, would receive a large share of all the gold that was found and all the money earned from trade.

Ponce returned to Borinquen in 1514. Florida, although unexplored and dangerous, now was his to govern. But he was unable to return and secure his claim right away.

In addition to discussing how Florida was to be governed, the king had appointed Ponce de León to command an armed force against the warring Carib Indians. The Caribs were terrorizing the Spanish settlements on the islands of the New World. Ponce was given an army to deal with the native warriors once and for all.

As before, the Spaniards succeeded in breaking the islanders' rebellion. But it cost many lives on both sides, and it took Ponce two years to win a shaky peace.

Even after the Indian uprising was settled, Ponce still could not return to Florida. He had to deal with jealous political rivals on the islands. The death of his friend King Ferdinand in 1516 also complicated things. With Ferdinand gone, was Ponce's Florida agreement secure? The soldier felt it necessary to return to the Spanish court to meet with the new king, Charles I. He was in Europe until 1518.

Even when he returned to Borinquen, there were too many obligations on the island to prevent his immediate settlement of Florida. Finally, by early 1521, he had equipped two ships for a second voyage to his new domain.

This time, he intended to establish a permanent colony. His company would carve out plantations in the wilderness and raise crops and livestock. Ponce intended to make Florida the most productive–and profitable–"island" in the New World.

By now, however, there were growing doubts that Florida was an island. The Spaniards had settled Cuba. They had sailed west across what is now the Gulf of Mexico to the Mexican mainland. Other explorers were probing what obviously was a great continent. They suspected Ponce's Florida might be an extension of it.

Ponce paid for the voyage himself. He promised his men both wages and land. There were tons of supplies, farm implements, and weapons to buy. He took livestock and crop seeds in order to establish plantations. He also took along missionaries, because part of the royal agreement was that Ponce must try to convert the Indians to Christianity. All this cost him a large part of the fortune he had amassed as a planter on Borinquen. But Ponce was convinced that control of Florida would be worth it.

His family would have to stay behind. Once a settlement was created and secured against possible Indian attacks, then they could join him. Many of his men also were married and planned to bring their families to Florida as soon as it was safe.

In February, the colonists set sail. As the caravels left Borinquen behind, Ponce gazed for the last time on the strange green island that had brought him both wealth and disappointment.

Ponce decided to sail up Florida's west coast to find a good location for his first settlement. The ships anchored in a sheltered bay. They waited to see if hostile Indians would appear along the shore.

This coast apparently was deserted, so Ponce ordered the men to begin unloading supplies. Sentries were posted around the beach. A party of men began looking for a place to build a fort. Scholars believe this landing place may have been near what today are Sanibel Island and Fort Myers, Florida.

On Hispaniola and Borinquen, Ponce had been able to overcome native resistance with military might and shrewd trading. But the Indians here, he knew from his earlier voyage, were different from the Taino. They had no interest in trading for the Spaniards' trinkets. Moreover, they did not seem to be intimidated by the Europeans' armor and weapons.

Several battles occurred at or near the landing site. The final one took the Spaniards by surprise. Indians sprang from hiding places in the high grass. They fired arrows and hurled spears from perches high above in the trees. They were everywhere!

The Spaniards fought back with cannons from the ships and with their swords, crossbows, and matchlock guns called *arquebuses*. They faltered, however, when Ponce was hit in the thigh by an arrow. His men carried him to a boat on the beach and rowed him out to one of the ships in the bay.

Today, a leg injury can usually be treated successfully. In the 16th century, though, medicine and medical procedures were very crude. They were even more primitive aboard ship.

Ponce's wound did not heal. Probably the arrow had a poisoned head. The leg became infected, and the infection spread.

The Spaniards sailed to the nearest settlement, Havana on the island of Cuba. Havana is 90 miles from the Florida Keys, and the battle with the Indians had taken place some distance up the coast—possibly a hundred miles or more. By the time the

While Ponce is remembered for his ill-fated attempts to explore Florida, his greatest accomplishments were on the small island of Borinquen, known today as Puerto Rico.

ship arrived at Havana, Ponce's condition was grave. Feverish and weak, he died several days later.

The conquistador's body was transported solemnly to his home on Borinquen. Today it is entombed in the wall of the San Juan cathedral.

While Juan Ponce de León discovered Florida, it

would be up to other Spaniards, like Hernando de Soto, to actually explore this lush new land. Although Ponce is often associated with the history of the charming old city of St. Augustine, Florida, it was Pedro Menéndez de Avilés who actually founded the city. That did not occur until 1565, half a century after Ponce's first Florida expedition.

Ponce's own great legacy is really on the island of Puerto Rico, which the Indians called Borinquen. There he built cities and did perhaps more than anyone else to establish European civilization. He is known as the "Father of Puerto Rico," and it is fitting that his body rests not on the coast of Florida, but in Puerto Rico's capital.

1460–1474   Juan Ponce de León is born, possibly in the Spanish town of San Servos.

1478   The Pope establishes the Spanish Inquisition, beginning three centuries of religious persecution in Spain.

1492   Christopher Columbus sails west to find the East Indies; in Spain, Ponce de León serves in the Spanish army as it defeats the Moors after a 10-year campaign.

1493   Ponce de León accompanies Columbus's second expedition across the Atlantic Ocean.

1502   Don Nicolás de Ovando is appointed viceroy of Hispaniola. In the coming years, Ovando appoints Ponce de León adelantado of the province of Higuey.

1509   Ponce de León explores the island of Borinquen (Puerto Rico) and is appointed island governor.

1511   Ponce is replaced as governor of Borinquen. For two years he devotes his life to his plantations.

1513   Ponce leads an expedition in search of Bimini. He claims what is now Florida for Spain.

1514–1520   Ponce makes at least one trip to Spain to ensure his rights as governor of Pascua Florida. He also leads a Spanish force in an island war against the Carib Indians.

1521   Ponce returns to Pascua Florida to establish a settlement. He dies after being wounded in a battle against the natives.

Glossary

adelantado–the title of a Spanish governor in the New World.

arquebus–a portable matchlock gun, invented in the 15th century. The arquebus was very heavy, and usually was supported with a wooden staff when fired.

caravel–a sturdy sailing ship developed by the Portuguese in the 15th century. Caravels had broad hulls, a high and narrow deck at the stern (called a "poop deck"), and three masts. They usually carried both square and triangular (lateen) sails.

conquistador–Spanish soldiers who led the conquests of Mexico, Peru, and America in the 16th century.

encomienda–a system by which land and natives were given to conquistadors and colonists in Spain's New World colonies; in return for the natives' labor, the landowners were supposed to provide them with food and a Christian education.

hammocks–a hanging bed made of netting. The Spaniards who came to the New World copied the Native American use of the comfortable hammocks.

heirlooms–an item of special value that is handed down from one generation to another.

immune–protected from disease. The natives of the New World were not immune to diseases carried by European explorers, so they were at greater risk of dying from the diseases.

infidel–a person who does not follow, or believe in, a particular religion. Muslims and Christians of the 15th and 16th centuries considered each other to be infidels.

maize–another word for Indian corn.

Moors–Arabs from North Africa who invaded Spain in the eighth century. Because the Moors followed Islam, they were involved in a series of bloody wars with the Christian people of Spain and the rest of Europe. The Moors were forced out of Spain in 1492.

page–a young attendant to a person of rank, such as a knight. Pages were often groomed to become knights.

plantation–a large farm or estate where plants and trees are cultivated.

province–a region of a country, usually separated from other provinces by geographical or political boundaries.

prowess–extraordinary ability or skill.

Spanish Inquisition–a movement during the 15th and 16th centuries to purge Spain of non-Christians.

spices–any of various aromatic vegetable products, such as pepper or nutmeg, used to season or flavor foods. In the 15th and 16th centuries, spices were rare and highly valued by the people of Europe.

squire–the shield and armor bearer of a knight–a rank above page.

viceroy–the governor of a country, who rules as the representative of a king.

Further Reading

Angelucci, Enzo, and Attilio Cucari. *Ships.* New York: Greenwich House, 1983.

Ballesteros, Manuel. *Juan Ponce de León.* Cincinnati: Aims International Books, 1996.

Blassingame, Wyatt. *Ponce de León, A World Explorer.* Champaign, IL: Garrard Publishing Company, 1965.

Dolan, Sean. *Juan Ponce de León.* Philadelphia: Chelsea House Publishers, 1995.

Dor-Ner, Zvi. *Columbus and the Age of Discovery.* New York: William Morrow, 1992.

Furlong, the Rev. Philip J. *The Old World and America.* New York: William H. Sadlier, Inc., 1951.

Fuson, Robert H. *Juan Ponce de León and the Spanish Discovery of the New World and Florida.* Granville, OH: McDonald and Woodward Publishing, 1999.

Humble, Richard. *The Explorers.* Alexandria, VA: Time-Life Books Inc., 1978.

Lobley, Douglas. *Ships Through the Ages.* Secaucus, NJ: Derbibooks, 1975.

Peck, Douglas T. *Ponce de León and the Discovery of Florida: The Man, The Myth, and The Truth.* St. Paul, MN: Pogo Press, 1993.

Index

Alaminos, Anton de, 44
Atlantic Ocean, 47, 48
Aviles, Pedro Menendez de, 58

Balboa, Vasco Núñez de, 44
Bimini, 41–42, 43, 44, 52
Borinquen (Puerto Rico), 8, 34, 35, 36, 37, 38, 39, 44, 47, 51, 52, 53, 54, 55, 57, 58

Cadiz, 21
Canonabo, 24
Carib Indians, 8, 53
Charles (king of Spain), 17, 53
Columbus, Christopher, 11, 17–18, 19, 21, 24, 25, 27, 29, 39, 46
Columbus, Don Diego, 39, 44
Cuba, 8, 54, 56

East Indies, 17, 35
Encomienda system, 31,

Ferdinand (king of Spain), 8, 16, 31, 36, 39, 43, 51, 52, 53
Florida, 8, 9, 47–49, 51–52, 53–58
Fountain of Youth, 41–44

Granada, 16, 17
Guaybana, 36
Gulf of Mexico, 48, 54
Guzmán, Don Pedro Núñez de, 12–16, 17, 18–19

Havana, 8, 9, 56–57
Higuey (province), 33, 36
Hispaniola, 8, 18, 22, 23, 29–30, 32, 33, 34, 36, 39, 55

Isabella (queen of Spain), 16, 18, 31, 43

León, Juan Ponce de
    birth and childhood, 11–14

death, 7–9, 57
and exploration, 21–23, 25, 29, 35–39, 47, 48–50, 55–57
and fountain of youth, 41–44
as a planter, 31, 33–34, 36
as a soldier, 14–16, 17
León (province), 11

Mediterranean Sea, 16
Moors, 16, 17, 19

Native Americans
    and diseases, 27, 33
    and farming, 31, 33–34,
    and fighting, 23–25, 26, 31–33, 38–38, 47–49, 53, 55–56
    and gold, 17–18, 23–25, 31, 35, 36
    and slavery, 23–25, 30–31, 33, 36
Navidad, 23, 24
Nina, 21, 45

Ovando, Don Nicolas de, 30, 31, 32, 33, 36, 39

Pacific Ocean, 44

St. Augustine, 47, 58
San Cristoval, 44
San Juan, 36, 57, 58
San Salvador, 46
Santa Maria de Consolación, 44
Santiago, 44
Santo Domingo, 27
Soto, Hernando de, 57
Spanish Inquisition, 12,

Taino Indians, 8, 30, 31, 32, 33, 55
Toro, battle of, 16

Vikings, 47

West Indies, 17

Picture Credits

DAN HARMON is a writer and editor in Spartanburg, South Carolina. He has written 13 books on history, humor, and psychology, as well as historical and cultural articles for scores of national and regional periodicals. He is managing editor of *Sandlapper, The Magazine of South Carolina* and editor of *The Lawyer's PC,* a national computer newsletter, and of *Law Practice Management,* a magazine published by the American Bar Association. His special interests are Christian and nautical history, folk music, and international correspondence chess.

AAW-4045